Sake in a Glass
Sushi with Your Fingers
Fifteen Minutes in Tokyo

Scott Shaw

Buddha Rose Publications

10 9 8 7 6 5 4 3 2 1

Printed in the United States of America

Sake in a Glass
Sushi with Your Fingers
Fifteen Minutes in Tokyo

Introduction

'84, what a year... The world was supposed to end; wasn't it? For me, the world began. '84 -- four year(s) ago. Seems like a lifetime...

I spend a good percentage of it; '84, (that is), out on the hard road -- deep in the foreboding realms of the non-civilized third world. A moment or three, however, was spend in far more accepting cultures and places; namely, Tokyo. I do love Tokyo!

These are some words, written in a brown notebook which I picked up there, (in Tokyo), on a late autumn afternoon.

Journeys, be as they may; they always begin and they always end. These words were taken from two (2) -- two of them. Journey's that is...

Beginning/end. End/beginning.

Life, it does go on and on and on and on; measured only by memorable moments. Here are a few of mine.

S.
88.1. November
Redondo Beach, California

one

7:23 PM
the time ticks away
as I wait
await
the time to go
go
into the night

       the moments
       they move
       as I write
       in a new notebook
       purchased in Tokyo

       take me home
       to-key-o

two

these pages
they feel different
like the napkin I used today
was like fingernails on a chalkboard

     I ate at McDonalds

the streets
they are the same though
the same as they are
the places
the same
as I have come to know

I broke down the wall(s)
I moved in

public transportation
the subway
move with the people
move through the people
move through the city
never seeing the city
moving via the underground
I arrived
and now here I am
merchandized world
match box apartments

I am glad I don't smoke
everybody smokes here
it is so stifling/so invasive
breathing in
other people's smoke

take it
a generation
that doesn't care
let's just throw it
all away

it is all the same
and all so different

three

last night
on the streets
there you were
Asian/Japanese
a beautiful lady

a lady
that I could/would
live all my fantasies through
and there you were
lipstick
long hair
clothing; modern
with a look that kills
just the way I like 'em

       call me suicidal

I walked by you
I glanced
you walked by me
you looked
but we continued

on our predestined/individualized path(s)
and all that is left
is this poetry

four

I want to take it
past the point
where I really don't give a fuck

right now
on my shoulder
a monkey climbs on my back

out here on the outskirts
life is not cheap

out here on the peripheries
every day cost a bill
a bill times a thousand
maybe
a thousand more

>dreams
>they don't come cheap
>living dreams
>well that
>costs even more

>a price worth paying
>but how?

my incoming
out here on the outskirts
none

      bills to pay
      throw them away
      I don't want
      to give a fuck

      if I want to live
      I can't give a fuck

flashback:
I want to travel up to
Santa Cruz
buy books that I never read
fuck that girl
who always stares at me
in *Cat and Canary*
travel the world
get drunk
fuck the women
live
as if there was
no tomorrow

      as for me
      I don't think that there is

I want to
not have to
have stupid psychological
head trips
in top of the line
five star hotel rooms

incoming bills to pay

>you know me
>I want to live
>the dreams that I long for
>and have not yet lived
>I want to know
>the dreams
>I have not even
>dreamed of yet

so tired of the…
stupid waiting/complaining women

>*"When are you going to come back to*
>*me?"*

>there they are
>over there
>scattered across the globe

and at home
back in L.A.
that is no home at all

no, I don't want to give a fuck
not about any of it

not about anyone
not anymore

sadly
stupid me
I do

five

hit the streets
there is nothing more to be gained here
here; in the hotel room

      only fantasy, unlived

      and television

      ah, Japanese television…

but to the streets
where the television
is lived
and the movies
forgotten

six

I walk the streets
in the Tokyo nighttime rain

I make my way
to this little night club

      arrival time
      maybe 9:15 PM

I mean, hey
I don't want to get there
too early
and isn't that about the time
that all night clubs
are opening up

but...
as it turns out
live music
6:30 to 9:00
whiskey and coffee
9:00 to 4:00

well, I guess
that is Tokyo law

so...
here I am

I decided to forget
the whiskey and the coffee

      the whiskey
      and the coffee
      open till 4:00 AM

      because I probably
      would have drank there
      till 4:00 AM

some how I am relieved
that I was able to walk straight
and find my way home
for it has not always been
that way

      I have been
      following my feeling(s)
      my feeling(s)…
      on this journey
      and it just feels right

      no intoxication tonight

      my feeling(s)
      and this journey
      took me to the subway

      took me to
      this music store

took me to
this sword shop
took me to room 2829
Tokyo Hilton International Hotel

I was out/out and about
outdoors into the night
outside the door(s)
of this little night club

I powered walked Shinjuku
seeing James Corburn
poster-ed cigarette ads
Matt Dillon's
shaving cream poster-ed displays

I was out
out and about
outdoors in the night
walked past a porno shop
it did give me a thought or two

whiskey and coffee
naked women
love and life
in the Tokyo night

I have been here before
many times before
with
no place

no one
left to be

seven

I think of my chick
back in L.A.
I think of my chick
as I walk home
  back to my hotel
  piercing the sky

  main and current
  L.A. babe

Spanish goddess
strapped/trapped in L.A.

I think of my chick
as my attachment to her fades
to distant colors
in this Asian night

  it has been so long
  that I have been out here
  so long
  that I have been gone
  long time gone from L.A.

I think of talking with her
I think of the too many times
we have had sex
sex the same way

god,
how I instantly
became bored with her
but yet…
she stayed around
but yet…
I have kept her around

like life
like most relationships
long-term in the no-term
they add up to nothing
boredom and nothing

I walk in the Tokyo night
I walk
bored with her memory

eight

in Bangkok
I could have fucked a whore
I was there last night
flew into TKO today

I could have
but I chose not to
lord knows
that has not always been
my choice

       my life
       it always loses itself
       between my self-imposed extreme(s)
       drunk and lust
       light and mysticism
       but don't you know
       that it all leads to the last
       case-in-point
       the shadow(s)
       of life's eternal quest
       for vision

in Bangkok
I could have fucked a whore
I was there last night
but I choose not to

at least not
last night
I choose not to

   me, I thought of
   my chick over in Korea
   who patiently waits
   for me
   I thought of
   what is to come
   what may come
   who she may be
   what I may be

   and no
   I did not fuck a whore
   in Bangkok
   no
   at least not last night

   but anyway…

I think back
to one of my drunken stupors
Saturday Jim
my buddy and I
riding our motorcycles

drunk
stoned
and flying like witches
through the night

we rode over to
North Hollywood
        Ventura Boulevard
where the whores were stationed at the time

        you know
        they periodically move
        move
        here or there
        due to police situations
        and all

Saturday Jim
he became Johnny Boy
he titled me
Jim Bob L. Rod

we found our prey
standing on a corner
and he went about negotiating with her
attempting to move her
down to a reasonable rate

"I don't want to buy it.
I just want to rent it for awhile!"

"Yeah baby, I know…"

finally, no dice on the offered price
we rode off
we scavenged the vicinity
scratched the night
only to find nothing
nothing to find
at least, nothing worth
          paying for

with our dicks
still firmly placed in our hands
we re-retuned

she gave in to the offered price
two for one

          nothing had tilted her monetary
          fantasy

          nothing
          no nothing
          no not anything
          not while we were gone

with negotiations concluded
into the back

of an old gray four door ford
we climb

    the coin had been flipped
    first me
    than Saturday Jim
    or should I say
    Johnny Boy

    he picked up my
    sloppy seconds
    sloppy thirds
    fourths
    fifths
    sixths
    who knows how
    her evening
    had been going
    financially speaking
    that is...

she was tall
black as night

she had a shaved pussy
she wore a wig

I remember little else
of what she looked like
of who or what she was

dark and the night
they merged
into their profound
suchness

lust
elixir
money
sex
blend it in
and only
one color remains

she placed a rubber
around my dick

she told me
if the po-lease-man
were to come
to tell him that I was her boyfriend

yeah, right
I thought
he's sure to believe that

she took my hard cock
she stuck it in her
she lay on her back
we fucked for awhile
in the back seat
of her old gray four door

she asked me
was I cuming yet
no, not yet…
we fucked a little more
she asked again

finally,
bored with the whole process
and too fucked up to cum
        cum
        at least any time soon
I told her now was the moment
here it was/there I was
when I said yes
she started to moan
moan as if she was really digging it
really getting off

        I laughed to myself

I played it out
pulled it out

in goes Saturday Jim
        when he's done
        he comes out all smiles
        whispering
        "I pulled off the rubber."

the whore
none too happy when she realized the reality
of this
      she found it
      laying on the floor
      of the old four door

"Johnny Boy,

     you son of a bitch!"
        she yelled
we get on our scoots
Johnny Boy and I

"Bye, babe..."

we ride off into the night
      rode
      filled with
      drunken laughter

in Bangkok
I could have fucked a whore
last night
but I didn't

in Tokyo
      tonight
I could have done the same
      but I didn't

call it age
        if you want to be specific
        I'm twenty-six

        call it mysticism
        any self-righteous fool   would
        call it anything
        I really don't care
        I call it nothing
        for that is what
                I got tonight

nine

I would like to go out
and dance tonight
I would like to go out
and sing
but desire keeps me here

       me
       locked
       in my
       hotel room bed

friday evening
I just don't want to waste it
I don't want to waste
any more life
       please god
       don't let me waste it
       don't let me waste it
       no
       not anymore

I would like to
stay out tonight

BE
with somewhere to stay
but desire
 keep me here

the desire for my misplaced/lost purity
     remember it?
     that was so long ago...

lost and alone
friday night

friday night
and my hotel bed

ten

lay me
on the railroad tracks
push me
over the edge
walk me
to the peaks of life
leave me alone
in the night

eleven

walk in the Tokyo rain
dance in the city's calmness
walk into
a crowded vision of umbrellas
and walk without one

    let the rain fall
    onto me
    wash my body
    wash my soul
    wash away the pain

dance in a different
rainy day vision
dance without the sun

live the moment(s)
of raindrop passion
    turn
    step left
    and exit
    the thinking world

    let the rain
    make me see
    that there isn't one

twelve

McDonalds
Shinjuku
I chance to go in
order two big macs
  feed me the poison
  feed me the food
  for the soul

next to me
over to my left
a woman
maybe young…
with her
it is hard to tell
  new wave clothing
  she orders a big mac
  I glance to my side
  and she smiles at me

  ah, the chance…
  the chance in the dance
with every dance
there is another chance

big macs
they aren't ready
  three minutes…
  so they say

I go upstairs
and wait

await their culinary arrival

soon
I see her
the girl
ordering a big mac
the one who stood next to me
the one who smiled

      her big mac
      also not in hand

she sits
in my field of vision
gives me
the glances of love
but what is there to say?
what can be said?

the big mac(s) come
hers and mine
      she similes
      at me
      I smile
      at her
ah, McLove
McTokyo love
in McShinjuku , McDonalds

how can these cards be played?

I play them as they are dealt

I finish my McBig mac
wait a McMoment
I get McReady
to leave McLeave

I go to throw away my McTrash
by where she McSits

>   as I pass
>   she had a mouth full
>   of big mac
>   but she still McSmiles

I thought that I would sit down
ask her if she spoke McEnlish
but with her mount McFull
I continued my McWalk

so
this McMoment is simply cast

like so many McBefore
to one of those glancing loves
out of the corner of your eye
that you know
could have been/should have been
forever and ever

but was not
it is simply lost
to these lost McWords
on this lost McPage
of distant McPoetry
written about my McTime(s)
in Tokyo

but, awh
it could have been great
I am left with the McFantasy

thirteen

I walk
through the subway station
    it is huge
I walk
as the Tokyo world
passes me by

coming the other direction
this total babe
of a Tokyo child
    lip stick
    flood pants
    her eyes
    they look directly
    into mine

me,
I'm feeling good/looking good
strutting by
with my long umbrella in hand
it tip-taps
makes music on the ground

    as I take each step
we are
eye-to-eye
heart-to-heart
soul-to-soul

ah, what I could do
with a woman like her

my dreams
they go into overdrive

you would think
I would be happy
happy
with what I have
in hand

one woman
waiting for me in Korea
another one
waiting for me in Spain

several other(s)
hanging onto the dream
that they may
        someday have me
        to themselves
back state-side

but love looks
and love kills
oh please
take my life here

        we pass each other
        as her glance meets mine

        we pass
        perhaps
        never to pass again

but the moment(s)
        of that glance
was worth a thousand
worn out
I love you's
from all those women
that I have had and have
and just do not care about
no, not any more

        a glance of passion
        a promise of
the unknown/the forgotten
those living like me
        lost in the unforgivable

that glance/that look
it is so pure in its essence
as it promises everything
        a promise
        that will never be known

I love the passing promises
of the everything...

fourteen

all day
everyday
standing
holding the elevator
when the elevator
would gladly hold itself

all day
everyday
"Good morning sir."
"Oh hi o go sai e mas."

all day
everyday
bowing
      constantly
      repeatedly
      what a job

elevator girl
dressed in modern
Hilton Hotel attire

all day
everyday
elevator girl
bowing

fifteen

hotel window
standing there
naked

twenty-eighth floor

do people look up and see?

sixteen

sitting here in the late night
nowhere left to run
walked past a night club
it was boppin'
like the club
thursday,
the week before

      no signs of new wave
      nothing even old

      old as the night
      life as it cries
      walk on
      depths of the streets

contact
contact is what I need

but contact
is so hard to find

contact with a feminine form

but contact
is not that easy sometimes

I guess the hermits

they have the right idea
no need for people
choose only to be alone

maybe that is their lie
I don't really know
but me
I want it
I need it
I just don't want to waste it

I guess it wasn't my time tonight
so I sit here
breathe in
rest awhile

then the streets
back to the streets
back out on them again

      with every dance
      there is another chance

seventeen

I am just walking the streets
nothing to see
nothing to be done
for I have done it
all before

I am just taking the night
taking it on
walking the razor's edge

but I can't give it up
no way/no how
I just can't give it up

no one to see
nothing to say
it has all been said before

nothing to taste
nothing to try
it has all gotten so old

I cannot listen to reason
       reason
       it doesn't mean a
       goddamned thing
don't want to hear the lie

as I sit here
in the corner
on the edge

the poison it kisses me
I love its form
the lover she talks to me
I close my ears
open my wallet
I do not want to hear
what she has to say

a moment in truth
equals the end of all lies

lust and life
kisses in the night

if the story was worth telling
if I could remember it
you know it would be told
too drunk
to even really remember

eighteen

is the night still hot
is there still
something to say
is your love still warm
than don't make me
go away

      dance little dancer
      dance

is there still
a second of reason
reason(s) that bind us
      to the night

if there is one more lie
than whisper it in my ear
keep me from the silence

      lie little liar
      lie

nineteen

I walk through
another saturday night alone
a saturday night
where are the beautiful
and more than available women
that I commonly find
       they are commonly
       but they are not common

I seek
an oh so fine form
it is just something that us guys
seem to do

but
the one(s) who have
met my stare
do you dare
why do you leave me here
all alone and dreaming
       I walk through
       another saturday night
alone

twenty

alone
and desire
turns to
love
and a form

at least
it always seems to
     in the case of me

love
and desire
the passion
and the fire

put yourself in the right place
and it always seems to come

inside the walls
they close in
close in
on me

place a psychic
energy net
around your face
and form
you wrap yourself

around me

help!
I can't breathe
I've got to get away!

don't your know better
than to fall in love
with a fool?

       just another girl
       on another night
       in Tokyo

twenty-one

I loved you best
when we are close
when I can look
deeply
into your eyes

I love you best
when all the doors
are closed and locked
so the world
cannot tell us how to feel

I love you best
when we are close
when I can see the movements
of your face
       every hair
       every imperfection
       every twinkle
       in your eyes

I love you best
when we are close

twenty-two

paradox
spiral spiritual reflex

how I want to love
and how I
        always
run away from it

where lies the secret
of my meeting every woman
every woman
who wants me
        wants me
        I want them
        but that feeling
        only lasts for a second
        having them
        I want them
        no more
                no-more

I want it all
I want them all
I want it now
I want to be in love
        forever and ever and ever
but forever for me
only last

a minute
      a second
            in time

I am so tired
of setting for
second best women
in a second best world
      my fault
      I know
I shouldn't let myself settle

settle and settlement
here today
gone tomorrow

      buy it
      return it
      I never want it
      too long

twenty-three

I have always
let myself get conned
into relationships

I rap my way in
with only intentions
for the moment
they wrap me up
package me away
put me
in the deep freeze
      and now
      it has
      happened
      again

the moment was great
the fantasy was lived
but a virgin
once removed
is no virgin
at all

everybody tells me
that I must learn
to compromise
that I must just take
what life gives me

take it
be happy
be satisfied
and settle down

but why?
I always wondered
where there is
        new dreams to come
old ones to relive
        a million women
        a billion chances
        and
        I want to take them all

twenty-four

my life
it has been funny
always the carrot
dangled
in front of my nose
eighteen
no need for a job
if I went to college
time lived well...
twenty-three
money from getting
my head smashed in
not enough
but enough for me to develop
champagne tastes
now what do I do
money is tight
and I am called out
by the night
love and life
women and *sake*
I want to live here
forever

twenty-five

sometimes you see them
women
who just say
WOMAN
all over them

lady
I want your number
     and your name

we passed in the subway station today
she walked by
staring at me
checking me out
as they often do
     I guess that they can't
     figure me out
     is actually
     the name of the game

long hair and earrings
baggy 1940's suit
long over coat and sunglasses
yes, I always wear my sunglasses

oh, how I love the ladies
the real ladies
classic style/classic looks

a goddess in formation
ecstasy for the taking
look
there she is
ga ga in love with me
but like
sitting on the dock of the bay
if I could meet 'em
I could get 'em
why don't I meet 'em
why can't I meet 'em
I must wait
wait
like all mystics wait
wait for the water to settle
settle into mud
mud
to dry dust
that blows away
in the wind

twenty-six

two robes
laid out on the bed tonight
two sets of slippers
awaiting upon the floor
one large
one small
and only me
here alone tonight

     it makes me smile
     smile
     in all the ridiculousness
     of life

twenty-seven

I go out of my way and call you
I go out of my way and see you
my second best woman
trapped in a first class world

and now where is it
where is the strength
which you have shown me

instead, I am met with indifference
aloof indifference
I hate indifference
       you say,
       your family
       surrounds you
       you say,
       they are listening
       to your every word

       you/like they
       speaks only
       a little English

I ask,

"So any new boy friends?"
only for a joke
my answer is silence

I ask,

"Do you still love me?"

just a little humor
       like I really care
       one way or the other
but not a sound is made

now where is the passion
the passion and the promise
smeared upon me
late in the evening last

now where is that love
that love
and that lie
that I would be your only
forever

if you cannot say it
in front of everyone
it was not worth saying at all

the world and this life
it comes down hard on us all
and if you do not want controversy
don't put yourself in controversial situations
       that seems to be the rule

       love and passion
       a promise in the night

am I not the only one
I guess not
I am not the only one
who lies
to get what is obtainable

people watching
so where is your strength

no holding hands
as we walk outdoors
I want to walk away

I go out of my way and call you
I go out of my way and see you
my second best woman
trapped in a first class world
but like most of them
      all of my flings
      that promise passion
      spoken with the words of
      forever
      you like they
      me like them
      it was not worth
      the waste of my time

twenty-eight

just a passing note
in a passing life
to my passing self
I go out again
passing
as I pass the mirror
I cast a passing glance
21 October 1984
my hair now looks
the way I wanted it to look
in and for Tokyo
when I started out on this journey
in February, I guess
though I have
 past this port
once or twice
it did not look this way
in April
it did not look this way
in May
but it does look this way
in October

Tokyo
ego
and life
ah, life…

64

twenty-nine

demons forgotten
lies never told
I wait for the moment
of movement
in the moment
I wait
for a shift

thirty

I have experienced
      loneliness
I have experienced
      walking the streets
people's eyes on me
but I was walking the streets
      alone

I have experienced
the never ending searching
      for truth
      love
      lust
      the answer
but I have searched for it
      alone

I have experienced
the need
      to always go out
      to find it
      to not waste it
      to run after it
      not let it
      simply come to me
      four walls
      breed nothing
      but insanity

I have experienced
the years of loneliness
punishment for a crime
I never committed
I have experienced
the running away
       from someone
       to nothing
       from nothing
       to no one
       for no better reason
       than belief
       that there must
       be something else
       something more
       far more worthy
       and far less used

I have experienced it
yes, I have experienced it
       all alone
for what does life hold
what were the promises
that were made
was it ever said
anyone is anymore
       than singular
where was it written
anyone lives for anyone
       but themselves

thirty-one

it is a funny state
while traveling
you have to be
out

      out
      to see
      to meet
      a chance
      in the dance
      no time
      for the nothingness

I remember
the time going slow
last winter
in Europe
and the Middle East
I wanted out
but first I had to get in

      out and in
      such a sin
      like sex
      a fool's poison

here in Tokyo
the time has gone
very fast

was it the
state of mind/state of time
          state of life
or just another daydream

thirty-two

I cannot quite
put the feeling(s) into words
how or why I go out searching
I go out seeking
especially in a place like this
Tokyo
drawn out of the walls
drawn out of myself
drawn out
by the overall beauty of the women
and there understanding
of the times
I need to meet one
one of those
a beautiful one
a perfect creature
prowling the imperfect night
take away my pain
take away my alone
give me
a fantasy
I need to meet one
I need to know one
I need a new one
not the second best kind
of vision
like the one that waits
around the last corner

the corner that I turned
as I walked away

but perfection
in and of
its own form

oh well…
just more tears
of a solitary poet
the tears
that so many have sung of before

thirty-three

I wonder
if I were to meet a dream
if I were
to be handed it
pure and simple
simple and sweet
all I had ever
wanted
would it stop me
could it stop
      my chasing
my fooling around

thirty-four

yesterday
walking in the rain
I moved quickly
to avoid a man
carrying a heavy load
       slip
       bam
       I wiped out
       on the Tokyo pavement

       I am glad
       that I know
       how to fall

interestingly though
interestingly even though
why?
I move to help a guy out
and it was I
       who wiped out

       was my ego too large?
       I don't think so

and besides
why isn't it OK
from time-to-time
or forever

to feel like your
looking good/feeling good
I mean I have done my time
on the opposite side
of that feeling
I guess it is the curse
        of the mystic
the damning of the saint
the opening of the eyes
        open isn't closed
        open can never
        be closed again
        and if you're dancing
        on the spiritual side
        of the path
        you have to expect
        the consciousness
                consequences

thirty-five

I take it
to this limit
I want to live it
all the way
I take it past its center
where there is
nothing left to say

    see you
    another time
    see you in my dream(s)
    see you
    in all my fantasies
    but fantasies
    are not the way
    they seem

    see you
    in another life
    see you
    in another time
    see you
    in a foreign field
    of vision
    see you
    when I learn how to feel

and there isn't any dream
that is not worth living
there isn't any dream
too small

      dream for it
      dress to suit it
      yes, dress
      the way you feel
      dream for it
      live for it
      and I will see you
      in the night time air

      see you in the night time
      in a sacred field of vision
      a view that is
      none to small

      see you again
      see you than
      when there is nothing
      no new to chase
      nothing left to lose
      and
      when
      I don't care anymore

thirty-six

there isn't any use in pretending
your love shows all around
isn't any way of forgetting
that you loved me
the way that I am

so hold me in your arms
try to make me feel
hold me on this rainy night
hold me
and let me know
that your love is real

       chain me down
       I will break the chains
       but give it your best shot

I can change my clothes
but you can't change me
child to man
man to woman
here I am
looking at you
seeing all you offer me
is all of the typical lies

let me jump
into your center

hide deeply in a hole
hide me from them
hide me from you
let me pretend
that you offer me something more
when I know that you do not

where will we go
where will you take me
someplace I am sure
that I have been before

　　stuffed animals
　　stuffed with lies
　　your lies
　　they are spoken
　　in your eyes

　　you have tired
　　but kiss me
　　goodbye

thirty-seven

fore-song
fore-play
in a 1960's mini skirt
left
right
right away
driving a Mazda car
count down
ten to two
I and you
and you and me
what are we going to do

spent the night
alright
I spend the day
OK

sing me your song
forget the time
for it is now
counting backwards to one

red shoe on
left one is off
and your songs
they sound all the same

turn around
you say no
I hate the word no
turn around again
and than
you say yes

fore-song
fore-play
in a 1960's mini skirt

you wrestle me to the ground
white is red
blue is green
I have had
what you have to give
and believe me
you don't have anything new
to be seen

thirty-eight

I looked at you
I even loved you
as momentary as love may be
I spoke with you
I listened to all of your tales
you took me to your home
you took me there
and wanted me to stay
       but lets face facts
       you are just
       a second best woman
       in a world
       with full-cn density
       a second best woman
       and there is just
       too many chances
       out there
       for me to stay

now you may be what I needed
needed for a moment
for we all know how needs
have the tendency to change

it is us
who chooses
to make life a fantasy
a dream worth living

a reason to die in the late night

but you just do not want me
to leave
so I sit here
staring out the window
you lying next to me
Tokyo lights below

      windows in the night
      and the allure they hold

and I wonder
what I can do
to get away from you
so I can go
and once again live
the win/lose
the gain/loss

the have and have not
the fantasy of the night

thirty-nine

it is funny
well, not too…
I'm sitting here
lonely as all fuck

      jump from one love
      into no love
      into the possibility
      of up coming love

tomorrow this chick comes
a local lady
I met her on a flight
Tokyo to Hong Kong
yes, awhile ago

      1:OO PM
      arrival time

      arrival time
      tomorrow
      l:OO PM

set for momentary fantasy
yet and yes
it could only be momentary
how long is long anyway?

but now
 I long for that momentary-ness
        something/anything

        again
        loving walks in the rain

I have been told
I spent too much time alone
but than I have been told
a lot of things

        one side runs away
        the other side longs

        just how long is long anyway

forty

I met with that chick today
that chick
Tokyo to Hong Kong

a lady of doubt
in doubt
who and what
is she

I met with her today
no chemistry

      when I saw her
      when I first saw her
      a lady stepping on board
      an aircraft

      one of those being
      that you pray
      will sit next to you

      a chance in the dance
      when any dance will do

      yes, I prayed
      yes, I remember
      how I thought
      that she may be

the most beautiful women alive

yes, I recollect
her teaching me
how to say
"I love you"
in Japanese

I lied
I already knew
how to say it

a phone call in Hong Kong
a return to Tokyo
a moment of nothing
based on a mind-full
of the possibilities

sad
dreams sometimes
add up to so little

possible love
as momentary
as that may be
a moment of talk
a moment of sightseeing
I had to show her around
her own city
a moment of nothingness
in another day gone by

a goodbye
at the subway station
she said
she would send me
a Christmas cards

so now everything
well, it all seems finished

finished this time around

how much love
can one expect from one journey anyway
so I guess it is time to go home

      home and life
      it is now October
      in November
      I will start out again

      home and life
      for a brief moment
      two, maybe three weeks
      at the most...

      than out and about
      around the world

the fast way
OUT

out
on the hard road again

and as for the chick
well, it could have been   everything
but I guess it was nothing
only a traveler's dream
on a wandering airline
lost deeply somewhere
at forty thousand feet
see you,
next Christmas card

forty-one

whispering daydreams
call me

mystical walks
in the fallen rain

eyes of a cat
face of the sun
the words
of the unspoken wind
become the clouds
overhead

sunrise sight
evening mind
I don't know why
but I fall in love with them
as I fall in love with you

forty-two

in a basic
give up and rest attitude
this afternoon
on my way out
    of the subway station
this beautiful
oh so beautiful
local lady
while moving her arm
gently touches me
in that special spot

    oh yes

then
just out of my hotel elevator
as I walk down the hall
a young maiden
nineteen-ish
is knocking on my door

"Housekeeping...."

I smile
I answer
I exclaim

"It is my room."

"Would you like me to
turn down the covers
on your bed?"
"Sure."

and as she finishes
and as she bows
I can see the obvious infatuation
in her eyes

should I/could I
I just don't know
I guess I will have to leave
this one
for some other
dreaming poet
who will be
far less worthy
than I
I am sure

then after dinner
tonight
still in the questioning space
I go down to the hotel basement
to buy two books
on my library list
as I leave the bookstore
the wrong elevator
I do take
not upstairs but outside

how can I do anything but
follow the signs

    the signs
    out
    to
    the
    night

I go out seeking nothing
which leaves
everything to be found

forty-three

within
four walls
it is easy
      only dreams,
      head trips,
       fantasy
the locked-in world
of another dream
never lived
never spoken
outside
I prefer it
where the chances
they become
so real

forty-four

words
they move into mystery
mind
moves into space
they left us
only lying here
left us
only life

oh, a lot of men
have called you mistress
a lot of men
have called you whore
but me
I call you heaven
and heaven
has lied to me

what you say
well, it means nothing
what you do
means no more
where you have been
well, it just doesn't matter
just slide
some of your violence
on me

whispered wisdom
it an open ear

forty-five

I asked for nothing tonight
but I got so much
I took a walk
I felt the evening wind
        of freedom
and realized
how much the buildings
block the ocean breeze

I asked for nothing
what I got was so much more
for the everything
sometimes
it comes in the form of nothing
and nothing
well, it means nothing more

Tokyo
the night
a walk
a peak experience
the wind being blocked
and Zen being found

forty-six

well, my plane
it doesn't leave until 6:15
I guess that gives me
another chance

how I love life
with every dance
there is another chance

I must stop all this seeking though
for you know
it does make me a little crazy

     searching
     for what?
     I always wonder
     well, I do have my list…

so dance in the chance
one more chance
and I may win
like any gambler
any junky
I think it will be
this time

forty-seven

ah, Tokyo
I love you

I mean
where else can I find
so many beautiful
new wave-ish
Asian women
who wear long skirts
love the fashion passion
and have a culture
so willing to
      break down the walls

no other Asian city, I think
not like Tokyo

ah, Tokyo
I love you

forty-eight

air turbulent

breath into the intensity

another shot
in the night

why

where does death
want to be life
when does a suicidal man
choose to live

cold air turbulent
streak through a winter's night

birth to death
death to life
the living live
the dying are dead
and the wind(s)
they gently sing

forty-nine

I want someone
waiting for me
at the airport
LAX
if you please
some love
but there is none
no one to meet me
the price l pay
for my lifestyle
is high

my choice...

fifty

it is funny
trying to make yourself sleep
when you are not even tired
solely for the reason
that you know you should sleep

sleep when tired
eat when hungry
drink when thirsty

live, when you can

fifty-one

I look at the seat behind me
an Asian lady sleeping
a tear is running down her cheek

next to her
an old lady, blind
maybe the mother
I do not know

their world...
perhaps their lives
    a reason to cry
    in their sleep

I cry for them
while I am awake

fifty-two

7:30 AM now
L.A. time
the city is waking up
I travel on this airplane
bound for home
such as it is

moving into new freedoms
freedoms of lost paradise
movement of mystic motion
where will it lead me to next

fifty-three

I sit here
a lonely poet
stretching out
onto his airplane seat
back against the wall
sitting up
staring into distant reason
seeking ancient ways
knowing today
was tomorrow
as I relive
yesterday

fifty-four

line for the bathroom
waits
almost to L.A.
"Must freshen up,"
they say

oh, how pretty
oh, how proper

pretty and proper
in an improper life

fifty-five

well, almost home; L.A.
forty-five minutes or so

no one to meet me
a momentary fantasy
that my main and current
L.A. Babe
will be there

every international journey
I have taken
real international journey
she has been there
to pick me up

but she is off in Spain
I am/was off in Asia

so on the return
this return
no one
I guess
to return to
and this time
I come back
with the most luggage ever
five luggage claim tickets
on my airline pass

to the sky
three of them
guitars

ah, life
the moment
the moment(s)
the world
the experience
the experience(s)

thank you god
thank you life
thank you for the chance
in the dance

www.ingramcontent.com/pod-product-compliance
Lightning Source LLC
Chambersburg PA
CBHW060419090426
42734CB00011B/2365